Observations of an Artist: Lived and Learned

A Spiritual Journey through Art and Poetry

Terry Spruell

Observations of an Artist: Lived and Learned

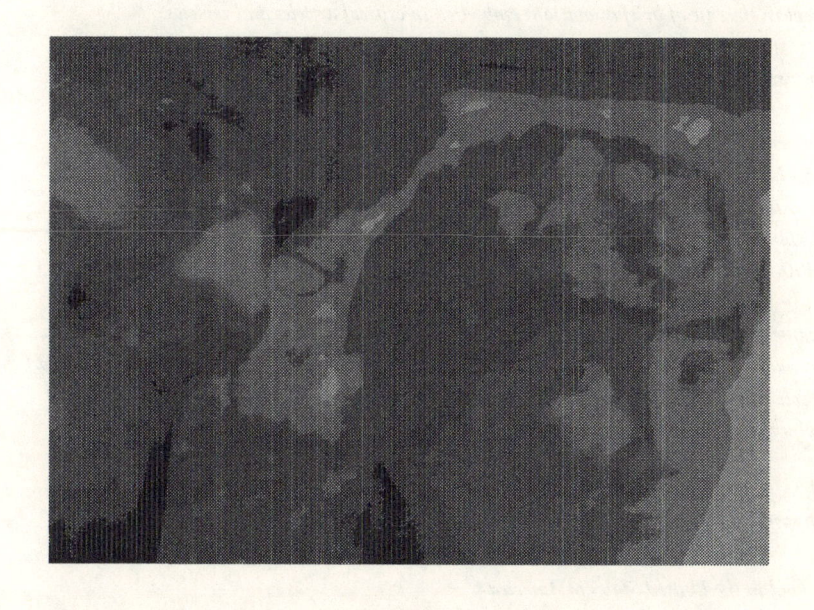

A Spiritual Journey through Art and Poetry

Terry Spruell

iUniverse, Inc.
New York   Bloomington

Observations of an Artist: Lived and Learned
A Spiritual Journey through Art and Poetry

Copyright © 2009 by Terry Jo Spruell

All rights reserved. No part of this book may be used or reproduced by any means, graphic, electronic, or mechanical, including photocopying, recording, taping or by any information storage retrieval system without the written permission of the publisher except in the case of brief quotations embodied in critical articles and reviews.

iUniverse books may be ordered through booksellers or by contacting:

iUniverse
1663 Liberty Drive
Bloomington, IN 47403
www.iuniverse.com
1-800-Authors (1-800-288-4677)

Because of the dynamic nature of the Internet, any Web addresses or links contained in this book may have changed since publication and may no longer be valid. The views expressed in this work are solely those of the author and do not necessarily reflect the views of the publisher, and the publisher hereby disclaims any responsibility for them.

ISBN: 978-1-4401-5643-4 (pbk)
ISBN: 978-1-4401-5642-7 (ebk)

Printed in the United States of America

iUniverse rev. date: 7/3/2009

Spend Time Creating with Word and Sketch

Do you want to understand the thinking of others? Through visualization and relating meaning to the physical world, God has given us the creative mind to see. Jesus Christ taught with parables. He knows we need to see and feel to get it.

You may be asking, "Why is this present time in life such a struggle?" At one point in my life I felt like a barren desert because I was unable to have a child. God gave me a view of White Sands National Monument in New Mexico that changed me forever.

Put in a place where only God knows my thoughts and disappointments, I came to Him through Christ. One step is seeing my need for Christ's love and forgiveness, but the other step is to believe God made me and has a plan for me. That plan includes bringing others to the knowledge of Him using the talents He has given me.

Therefore, a book to encourage others to be still, to wait, and to take notes on what is being said by friends and family came to my mind. A career of teaching and sharing with others gave me a view of people and how people communicate, which helps to make sense of the world. Now I make you an offer: come with me, visit over a cup of coffee, and make sense of our world.

God says to "Be still, and know that I am God" (Ps. 46:10). God wants you and all who will listen to come aside spending time to drink of water that will satisfy like no other.

About the Artist

A tomboy with a name to prove it, I grew up on the farm in Splendora, Texas, with loving parents and a close-knit family. I spent my Saturdays riding my horse from morning until dusk. Since those carefree days of youth, I have chosen God to be my Lord each day.

Contents

I. Places 1
White Sands; Seasons of a River; A Summer's Morning in Winters, Texas

II. Relationships 9
Two Voices; Pocket Watches; Three Actors; Joana; My One and Only; Ring; Who Are You? The Friend, the Mirror

III. Nature 29
A Leaf Fell Down; Bees Living Free; Trees Bend and Sway; Owl; Line

IV. Choices and Circumstances 41
Fact of Life; Serpent Question; Chair in Waiting; In the Dark; Doorway; Crisis; Vote; Students

V. The Ultimate Relationship 59
Heart, Soul and Mind; You Made Me to Think; Truth Freedom's Key; The Love Letter; Do You Know; Music; A Song

Places

White Sands

Why was I created? To dramatize the travel of the unseen wind or stir under its hand?
Some term me barren, but they do not know the plan.
Some gaze upon me and think I am only sultry and seared.
They have never experienced my night or reached down into my depths.
Those close to me know I am constantly moving;
why and where, that is not for them to discern.
I know the mountains hold me, but if the wind should decree it,
I would move to the other side, one grain at a time, ever so slowly.
Drizzle comes down upon me. My surface retains its mark,
the alkaline and gypsum make-up fashioning crystals in response to the cool touch of the rain and then the heat of the sun.
Other portions of me are smooth and unblemished
and anticipate the wind, who will move my heaviness particle by particle.
I consider my creation; does it give my heavenly Father delight
as I move ever so slowly one grain at a time?
Time is His, and He knows my every portion,
From the smooth, rounded surfaces, to the crystals upon crystals that form in response to the elements of rain and sun.
God almighty grants the wind, sun, and rain.
He knows my nature. The refreshment I give the white lizard in the heat of the day as he burrows deep within my moist white sands.
They that stay on top and cannot bear the heat and cold
must move away and view my loveliness only for a while.
They that go beneath the surface know relief;
they adjudge me a friend.
See me only in passing, or take hold as I move ever so slowly
beneath my Master's hand. Change is a part of every day
As the unseen wind forms and shapes me.

Place to Draw:
What should you put in the foreground just below the edge of this desert landscape? Footprints or a buried canteen seem like a good choice. Remember, when adding in an object that the light source is above, shade the shapes to create depth and form.

Place to Write:
Go ahead and ask the questions about those desert places of your life. Put the words down and listen. Be aware of all that is around you, such as that mockingbird singing his little heart out even though day after day he seems to be alone in the tree tops without a mate.

Seasons of a River

The dry river bed is waiting. When will the season come for its
filling?
Remember the storms that brought torrents of water
rushing, gushing to the river's banks.

The muddy waters pushed all the litter before it.
Then the sun shines and the birds sing.

Now see the clear, flowing water moving over shiny river rocks.
They glisten beneath the tête-à-tête of the waters.

What is the water saying? "Refresh your horse and
cleanse your face …
but there is more to be had here."

All the day's exchange is distant as one hears the splashing, cascading rapids.
A concert, a hymn of love and hope, is rendered
in this place.

There are seasons of dryness
that receive the storm and have things torn away.
Floating by, the collection forever changes.
The days come when the river runs clear and laughs again.

Receive the waters as the dry river bed:
waiting for its neighbors and hoping for the water of life to fill it again.

With my mount refreshed,
my face moistened,
and mind made clear,
I meet my season of change.

Place to Draw:
Overflow the lines of the landscape and river beyond the boundary of the picture with a black pen or soft lead pencil. Use a system of lines that intersect to create action. This technique is called cross-hatching.

Place to Write:
List the things in your life that have been swept away. Have you been able to live without them? Have you let the past go? Celebrate the letting go and move on to the next shore of life.

A Summer's Morning in Winters, Texas

Six AM, the moon still shining, a few stars still visible. The curtains flap with a cool morning breeze. Can't sleep, have a need to explore this landscape seen only by headlight the evening before. Start down the hill along the clay and rock road toward the highway at least a mile away.

A rustle of grass, then a white tail flies into view over high fence; this is all that is recognized of the deer. Off to the southeast, a line of clouds hurry across the sky. These dark clouds, caught by the break of the morning sun, appear to burst into flames, swirling and boiling, bright with pinks, oranges, and blues in a magnificent display around the bottom edge of the great glowing orb of this new dawn.

To earth again my attention is drawn when something jumps into view on my right. Is it a jack rabbit? No. Another deer, small in the distance, is unsure about what to do as it bounds across to the left, darting, stopping, and finally dashing at full speed out of view without a sound.

A feeling of reverence and of privilege keeps me from going further down the lane turning before the first farm house. Jogging along, I don't want to be noticed—not by humans.

Flowers of all kinds: pretty blue, dark blue, with yellow middles, white, violet. Tiny, tiny flowers all bunched together, looking as if the petals will blow off at any time. "Pick them to press," comes the urge, but then the thistles I see. Thorns and cactus flowers, they remain for others to see.

Place to Draw:
What is missing in this picture? Sketch is a stroke or two to indicate a fleeing animal and then add scribbles to make a rabbit or white-tailed deer. How about adding the silhouette of a home with a light on in the distance?

Place to Write:
The next time you wake up unable to sleep, ask God to talk with you. What does He tell you?

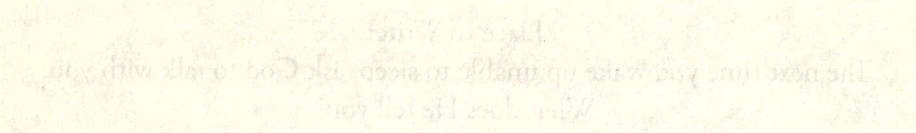

Relationships

Two Voices

Two strangers meet in a bookstore coffee shop, one with a need and the other oblivious to all but the quiet peace, until in this state she perceives the first, the sad needy person staring at a picture of the Grand Canyon. She smiles at the scene and is caught looking by the other. Hoping to bring joy to a sad person, the intruder says to the canyon admirer,

God has made some big beautiful places! And even so, He is bigger still.

God is bigger?

Yes, He must be!

How can that be?

Look at your hands.

No hands here ...

The God Person notices that the two arms of the Canyon Admirer are absent of hands.
Without even a blush, GP replies with an honest smile,

Okay. I noticed your eyes first, and you don't have a mirror ...
So look at your heart.

The CA points to her chest and, responding to the sincerity of the GP, says,

Keeps me alive but it is hurting and empty.

God made it to be full.

Then bring it on! *CA says with a hint of anger.*

Of course you have asked Him to, right? *GP is still without fear.*

No, why would He listen to me? And I don't even know Him.

You don't know me.

You I see and hear!

This longing to be full is just as real as me.

How do I know this is true, real?

You miss your hands and all they could do; your heart misses His presence.

Both strangers are unaware of others in the present world and smile at each other as they move toward a table with two chairs. The CA's eyes tear up in response to the courage and conviction revealed in the GP's replies to her need.

Now shall we talk with God together at this table?

Your heart can help me talk with God.

GP retrieves her New Testament from her backpack. The first lesson of many happens that day at the bookstore between the two new friends.

Place to Draw:
Color the sky bright blue and the balloons complimentary or analogous colors, such as orange, yellow-orange, and red-orange.

Place to Write:
Mankind has not always known how to fly. Put on paper what you would like to over come and what you think it would take to get up above it to see it from another perspective.

Pocket Watches

Pocket watches, twenty to twenty-five, ticking each with its own unique sounds. My brother Vance tells me that the tick of each watch is individual to that watch. The reason for this, he explains, are varied: the type of material used to make the case, the thickness of this material, the size of the parts, the case, and on and on it goes.

Vance derives much pleasure in collecting old and new pocket watches. He has information of interest as to why he values each, and the stories are entertaining. When the owner is present to tell his stories of how he obtained his watches, viewers spend more time admiring them. These little machines of time are attractive, but with Vance's enthusiastic presentation, these watches are most captivating.

Alone with the timepieces displayed in my glass-topped coffee table, I give them each five twists of the stem to bring them to life just as Vance instructed. I lift one to my ear and listen. Warm thoughts of the past come to mind and heart. My mom winds a Baby Ben to put in a shoebox with the newborn bird found on the ground far from its nest. She explains that the ticking will soothe the baby, allowing it to sleep. Surely the working of this woman's heart gave me comfort before and after I was pushed into this world.

The rhythmic click and tick is a sound of peace even though it is metal on metal within a cold vessel of nickel, brass, or steel. How much more peaceful is the sound of a human heart keeping time second by second, moment by moment, year in and year out.

My brother appreciates the fine work involved in putting together the pocket watches, and this causes me to delight in the One who put together my heart. I visualize my Creator drawing me up to His ear to listen to His handy work. Yes, He knows the unique tick of my heart, and He rejoices in it.

I wonder what kind of watch I am for my Lord: an everyday watch or a display watch. I want to be an everyday watch, smooth from use and always nearby. Of course the Maker has no need for a timepiece, so the analogy goes no further. Even so, will I let others know that the time is now, the time to come to Christ? Unlike the watch, I can choose to be set to the beat of my Creator.

Vance, my brother, I thank you for allowing me to examine your watches. They have given me much to think about.

Place to Draw:
The chain is missing on one of the watch fobs. Find it and sketch it in lightly with pencil. Use a pattern of rectangular boxes to create the chain. Finalize in pen.

Place to Write:
Describe your concern for another. Be ready to express your heartfelt care for that person's welfare. Ask Christ to show you how to love this person. Be ready to speak truth to another in the name of our Lord.

Actors: The Artist Megan, the Barista Sally

A quiet night at the local coffee shop. Megan hangs out to sketch and drink coffee. She is a people person who enjoys using her God-given talent of encouraging others. At times it is a child or teenager who is entertained with quick sketches of cowboys, Indians, and galloping horses. At other times she draws portraits of those who sit unaware that they are the subject of a detailed pen drawing. The baristas are familiar with the habits of this regular customer and they seem to enjoy characters of all sorts.

The weather is beautiful with high clouds scattered in the blue sky. A southern wind off the gulf keeps it cool, not too cold or hot. The first day of spring was a week ago. The music selection is from the '70s ballad era, easy to listen to.

Sally is about to take her break, and the artist has promised to do a quick sketch for her to keep. Megan has looked for opportunities to share the truth of God's love and desires to have a personal relationship with all people. In her life, this fact has kept her at peace. "I Am a Rock, I Am an Island" twangs in the background a song from the sixties.

Megan remembers her heart singing these words, first with pride and then with fear and loneliness. How far she has come since the times of rebellion. Now in her fifties, she still has times of loneliness, fear, and disappointment. During these times she is not without peace and comfort because her relationship with God allows her to deal with them.

"Hey, I am ready to sit and relax while you slave away at trying to make me look good." Sally's chipper voice brings Megan back to the here and now. Megan just smiles in reply. As she begins to lay in bold strokes of her subject's features, Sally, with a bit of self-consciousness, asks, "What goes through your mind as you draw?"

How would you answer?

Place to Draw:
What is missing? Add items such as coffee cups, newspapers, and computers to complete this scene. How about people? Visualize people as letters of the alphabet, numerals, or links of sausage, with each section of the sausage a bend of the knee or elbow. For example, the number two (2) could be a person under a table trying to unplug a computer power cord from an outlet.

Place to Write:
Someday you may find that you have time to do things you never thought you would. Be prepared for those times by dreaming now, so that you have a plan and the best is not taken by the good. God has a plan for your life, and it is the best. Let Him speak to you daily about His plans.

Joana

Glad, delighted—that depicts my colleague, my friend. Satin bronzed skin wearing a grin that radiates so brightly. Glowing so warm with sincerity and interest, she seems to want to experience what is within life.

On first meeting this gentlewoman of gaiety, I found her probing with skill and tact for getting beneath my skin. Does she know that God has given all of us a segment of Himself?

With caution I found myself meeting her gaze and pondering, "Does she want truth or cotton? Does she see me or spun cotton?"

Then I wondered whether she, like me, had come to the somber truth of opportunities expired and lost desires? Could we speak of God's favor and compassion?

On the façade appears softness and patience. I know the fury within my soul, a place where only God can bring calm and peace.

Have you ever met a person you felt you could let in? In my weakness, God is strong. My weakness will be the life of me, and it will not be me but Christ in me.

Joana, have you seen the part that brings pain and discomfort? Have you walked slowly over the ground of your heart?

Is that why we have talked so quickly about things of depth? Can we talk of a mutual walk, an eternity of finding our Friend, our Lord, and Christ?

Place to Draw:
Draw a face in the oval and use the lines for the
proportions of eyes, nose, and mouth.

Place to Write:
What is in a face? Looking into the eyes of a child, one sees so much of what is going on in that little life—that is, unless that child has been hardened by life. Do you know friends or family that will not look you in the eye? In some cases it is a cultural thing, but in others it is a deep need for love and understanding that only Christ can give. Write a prayer here asking for eyes that are Christlike and allow others to let you tell them of His love for them.

My One and Only

No one knows me like you do. No one cares for me as much as you. Oh, you don't know me to the depths that my God does, but I believe you know the sum of all that I am. Where can I go to find an ear that hears as well as yours, eyes that see me straight to my heart in good times and bad? My friend and lover, to no one else are these names combined. I trust your touch, whether in word or skin to skin. My husband, my princely priest, you have loved me as Christ loves His bride the church.

Place to Draw:
Design a leaf outfit for Adam and Eve. Remember that they just learned about sin and that they are naked.

Place to Write:
Write a description of how you felt when you first realized that sin was in your world. When did you understand that you are a sinner? How did this come to you? Are you allowing Christ to reveal to you daily your need for cleansing?

Ring

Let it *ring*!
Steve, you are my husband, and I'm so proud of it.
Ring,
In the spring of our engagement, all I could do was buzz with anticipation!
Ring,
Now, in our autumn, there is so much to take me through the winter.
Remembrances
happy and sad; we worked together through the lean times and the mean times,
through dreams lost and successes fulfilled.
No matter; in God we found our fill.
Ring,
The original ring is gone, lost at this time.
Even so,
Ring,
my heart knows the place I have been put,

placed and held by your prayer before the Father.

These new rings are not to replace but simply to celebrate
anew the love we share together in Christ.

Above and below are circles of gold
keeping the woven bands together just as Christ's love has kept us together.

Thank you, my love, for being my priest before the Father.

Place to Draw:
Color each ring gold, for they symbolize a precious union.

Place to Write:
How do you plan to nourish yourself? How will you encourage others to come to Christ?

Who Are You?

You see me as I want you to see me—
or actually who I claim that I am.

Now, I want to deal with who I've found I am.
Will you join me, my confidant, my friend?
You look as if you've never seen me.

It is interesting, bizarre, tragic:
you view me with a look of suspect,
as one who looks at a stranger,
and yet I've never been this honest.

Being who I was meant to be is new to me and less
labor to insist.

I say good-bye to the one who is my creation,
And hello to the friend, the Creator that made me.

Place to Draw:
The curling in of the patterns of this composition creates movement and space. By following the curved lines, continue the shape outside of the border.

Place to Write:
Instead of working on a self-identity, work on your Christ identity. How are you letting Christ show through you? Romans chapter 8 inspires one to live in life. Read and response here.

The Friend, the Mirror

The friend, the mirror, is a friend to receive or not receive? Is it to reflect or to shine?

Does the person before you reflect your image or shine back an image she wishes to see?

The mirror does not need to speak, it reacts to an image in the light not in the dark. A friend can not be untrue to its purpose of reflecting an image in the light.

To be water for the thirsty soul is to quench the need. To be anything else is to heighten the desire. Only one true liquid refreshes the human cells.

A friend is like water to the soul. But Jesus is the only well that will fill the need of you and me.

Communicate

In this relationship with the mirror, truth is seen…avoid this or consider how to relate.

How can we best reflect when our surfaces are distorted and deformed by sin?

Stand before me, Christ Jesus; communicate with others so that they may see You!

ENEMIES
LUKE 6:27

Place to Draw:
Draw a mirror and put it in your make-believe dream house.

Place to Write:
Write a detailed plan of a house you would like to have. If given the choice, would you do what it takes to keep it up and running? With rewards there are responsibilities. Freedom must be protected, health is a gift, and life should be lived. What do we mere mortals control? Give your life now to the Creator, Christ, the Alpha and Omega.

Nature

A Leaf Fell Down

An oak leaf fell onto the water's surface. It was pleased to see its reflected top side as it glided down. To see for once in its life, even at this late stage an image of grace. For falling from the life-giving tree meant death and returning to the earth to become mulch or some other sort of debris.

Now this leaf could see himself as an individual with curls and tucks not matched by any other oak leaf. Sure, oak leaves had come and gone, but no other was this exact shape or pattern of color.

Only by the water's power would this natural object of beauty move and have an image.

Wonder was in the heart of the leaf. The thoughts and hopes of this dying thing could be heard by the stream. With a ripple and a gurgle, the stream spoke to the undulating being. "I am glad you enjoy what I see and reflect back to you, but I cannot turn you over so that you may see your back."

At that moment a gust of wind lifted the leaf as if to say, "I will help you," for many times leaves have given the wind a voice.

Seeing the underside of its own form was a delight to the aged leaf. From stem to vein, the silky smooth texture was a surprise to its owner.

On and on the journey went until one day the leaf was left upon a clay riverbank. Here the leaf was sure it would dissolve, becoming one with the minerals in the clay. Not this time. This leaf was meant to be a reminder for others to see for many years to come.

Even though the elements of the leaf did join the clay, its unique image, its shape, even its texture was forever imprinted on the fossilized clay.

Place to Draw:
Draw a box giving it sides so that it is a cube and sketch eyes looking out of it. Label this shape my view of God.

Place to Write:
List the times you have been surprised by God. If you cannot think of any, ask God to surprise you and get ready to have a list.

Bees Living Free

One summer day without much display, bees show interest in the "ole smoky" pit.
Ole smoky is not being used as it sits under the porch away from rain and wind. The bees see it as a place to bring into "beeing" offspring and plenty of honey.
With an easy view from the dining room, I watch a display of industry underway for several days.
The lid to ole smoky is off a bit, allowing entry in the middle. The air inlets on top and bottom are open, too, providing air flow for the nursery.
Bees are industrious and are wonderful in the work they do. In and out they go, more than a half dozen delivering pollen from the neighbor's blooming crape-myrtle.
With reports of bee colony collapse syndrome, responsibility for the whole of bee future weighed heavily on my mind.
What to do!
No one will come to save these bees without a fee.
With some reasoning from my husband, I admit these bees must not settle here. Now to discourage colony making, a pole is needed.
With a ten-foot pole the lid is lifted—oops. Another pole with more rigidity makes the lift.
The lid is heavy. Several pushes, and it topples and rolls, revealing five sections of combs filled with crape-myrtle honey.
In the yard and opened to the hot sun, the bees freely move until it's plain that their combed store of babes and food cannot be saved.
They all fly away leaving a treasure of future bees and honey energy.
Not one sting is delivered, not one swarming bee is killed in the making of this colony or in the moving.
Bees and me, we live free.
Some other will enjoy their industry!

Place to Draw:
Scribble a few bees in, remembering that in flight it is difficult to see their wings. Bees in the distance will have little detail. The closer the bee is to the viewer, the more detail that will be seen.

Place to Write
Reflect on a time when you worked with others and it seemed that everyone knew what they were supposed to do.: Could it have been when you and others helped at an accident scene by directing traffic or calling 911?

Trees Bend and Sway

After a day of storm, ruin in its wake.
It looked grim.
The wind and rain loosened the anchors of the mighty and the small.
Beneath the earth, one is unable to see the roots, the system, and the grid—a maze webbed in such away that these trees have stood for many years,
to the delight of many a traveler, settler, and inhabitant of this land.
Would it be the oak or the slender pine that would succumb to the disastrous binge of storm rage?
In the eye of Ike, we ventured out to see what was left of each of our beauties.
To our surprise most looked fine.
Back into the safety of our house—to the hall, the closet, the shower, or the tub—to brace for the turn of the winds to come.
At the backside, the front side's terrible twin was louder, and the winds were more forceful yet to blow. "Wait and see" is all we humans could do against this force of nature's power and rage.
September
passed, and it is almost November. Slowly the uprooted trees are cut up for fuel for barbequing and winter warming at the fireplace.
"Normal" is a view with fewer trees,
these trees made into new memories.

Place to Draw:
Add leaves to these trees and more plant life in the open spaces. Think about adding repeated patterns.

Place to Write:
Are there patterns of behavior in you life, good, bad or indifferent? List them and see what it shows you.

Owl

Early daybreak,
Late afternoon,
And night—
These are the times I choose.
When the glow is blazing,
I am not to be noticed.
All I yearn for is sleep.
In the night, I see finest:
Shadows Are no puzzles for one like me.
Black and white,
Contrast I comprehend.
Movement is easy to detect,
And I measure promptly what it means.
The transaction of subsisting
Makes me keen.
Patiently, steadily, and quietly
I patrol.
Those who are not insightful
Overrun me as I stand,
An unblinking
Sentinel
Ready for command.

Place to Draw:
How many owls do you see?
Add a few of your own creation in the distance.

Place to Write:
Think about the gifts and talents you have and list them. If you can't think of any, ask the Lord Creator to show you today! Don't forget to write them down.

Lines

In the trained hand of the artist, lines of black trace visions of imagination. With an eye for shapes arranged in a pleasing pattern, the illustrator guides the observer to the point of interest.

Girded space, forming patterns of interest, are placed—and for what purpose? Is it a plan of a future place of dwelling, or an illustration of a character in a story?

Lines in black and gray,

simple and basic, creating fantastic shapes of beauty. Lines flow over and through …

Time line
Bottom line
Life line
Line of sight
Fine line

True and precise, that is the line.

That is why I like to play with lines.
Used correctly, it communicates dimension, space, place, and more.

Place to Draw:
Using a straight edge, begin drawing lines. Practice making lines with a very sharp pencil point, pressing down lightly to make faint marks. Allow some lines to intersect at various places along another line to give the overall composition interest. See what you create when diagonal lines are added to the intersecting points.

Place to Write:
Take time to write a thank-you note to someone special in your life. Be sincere and put effort into this.

Choices and Circumstances

Fact of Life

One day, the fact of my life strikes me oh so clearly: I was living less than I was created to be. I only lived what I thought I could be. At this point, a person afraid to live, I can see. "This is me!"

I held onto my desires so they wouldn't take me over or be taken—and they held onto me. So, this bright, clear day, I throw them away, not into space but back into my Master's hands.

These things I thought originated with me, but in fact they were put there by my Creator. Having taken them and made them what I thought would give me the most of each desire.

Now, I see, as I release them back to Christ, that He made them fit this new creature. Now every morning there are these desires, along with His faithfulness. New desires under the control of the Creator and King.

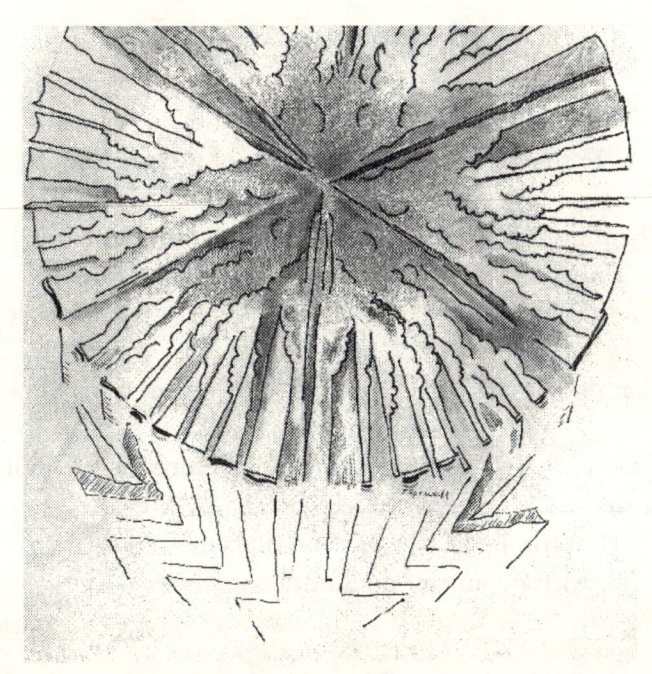

Place to Draw:
Use a straightedge and draw lines from a center point to form a radial design. Move the paper, not thinking of top and bottom in the design stage. After a full circle is made, begin adding organic lines. Organic lines are what would be seen as the edge created from white foam against a black cup, or a white cloud against a dark blue sky. At this point, begin to add more lines to the side of the design that is heavier visually; this will be the bottom of the design.

Place to Write:
What are the facts of your life right now? No matter good or bad the circumstances of life change. Hang on by reviewing the good times during the bad.

Serpent Question

Questions can plant doubt.
"Ye should not eat of every tree of the garden?"
The woman answers No.
The foothold is established, the seed of doubt planted.
The Serpent questions anyone who will respond.
"Are you pleased with what you have?" or "Do you have all you need?"
What does a snake have for you? Skepticism is his hook, complacency his nest.
You choose who to converse with today. From the first waking moment to the last thought as sleep overtakes, will you listen to the promise keeper or the doubts deliverer?
The certain answer does not need a query; He is.

Place to Draw:
How do you see the tempter? Coiled, ready to strike, or sunning and waiting for the night? Draw what you believe is the outward appearance of the serpent.

Place to Write:
You cannot reason with a liar, so beware even going there. Instead, agree with God right here and now. Write scriptures here that guarantee what God says about those who have allowed Him to make them new.

Chair in Waiting

Look, here is a place to sit awhile.
The cool, hard plastic is covered
By a rug of blue, natural white, and light green strips.
Before the outdoor chair is a jug of bubbling water,
Set high on limestone rocks that were put in to make a restful view.
Here time is used to reflect and manage the screaming of the everyday life.
Gray cat, what have you to do with this place, with not a care or use?
Why, you will leave hair on my rug.
You are a stranger in these parts.
Up you go with a start!
With the turn of the rug, my place is ready for use.
Oh, the things to be learned from the life of a cat.
Felines know how to be still.
Why my yard? Is it because I have no dogs or cats? That's the clue.
This chair is not used enough to keep a cat away, so hey, what's the rub!
Use it or lose it to an opportunistic cat.
Could it be that this cat knows how to handle the stress of life?
Here is a show of wisdom for me: give yourself time to be quiet,
enjoying the simple pleasure of stillness.
Do not be afraid to relax the brain to dream first before analyzing the
approach to the goals of the day.
Need help dreaming? Read Hebrews, chapters one and two, allowing
all the worries and stresses that clamor for space in the waiting chair
to find their place.
The First and the Last will tell what is to be the goal of the day.
Did He not create the day and night? Yes!
Cat, your name is blessed!
Blessed you and I are under His feet.

Place to Draw:
Add a scribbled black kitten of your own. Begin by lightly drawing an outline with pencil and then using a black fine-point pen. Then scribble in the rest of the shape by taking into consideration that some areas, such as eyes and shiny fur, need to remain.

Place to Write:
Watching animals is something I got hooked on long ago. Just for fun, try it and see what God teaches you! Record your experience here.

In the Dark

When I was a child, I sometimes
feared the dark.
Now, I see it as a confidant.

I can go in, eyes opened wide,
but there is no radiance to
reveal my inactive state.

I go there to be … just be. The blackness
at one time was suffocating; it is now a
place of consolation.

I breathe slowly and recognize peace
that is tender and all encompassing.

How could I go into this total darkness if not
for the charity of Christ? Yes, He is there with me!
He said there was no place
His Comforter would not advance.

My alienation from the light of day
is nothing compared with the darkness my
Savior saw as He died upon the tree.

Now, with my Christ, I share the light
of the Father's smile,
love and fulfillment Christ brought with His death on the cross.

I encounter each day knowing that God,
in His love,
meets all my questions.
I know Him, my Master and Lord, over all.
That answers everything.

Place to Draw:
With a soft lead pencil, shade in the shapes above with a variety of values. Number the shapes that appear to be on top as "1" and the shapes overlapped by top shapes as "2" (or "3" if they are under the first layer and the second layer). When the numbering is complete, shade with light values first. Work with pencil or pen. Think about how your eyes adjust to darkness when just a small amount of light comes in to a dark place.

Place to Write:
Fear is real and often gives us the sense that we need to escape danger. At other times we need to take it apart with a list that shows us what is real and what is imagined. "Come, let us reason," prophet Isaiah spoke in relationship to sin. Is sin causing you to fear?

Doorway

Doorways are to go through ... when one is ready to
proceed.
The doorways of life are only for going in
beyond yourself.
Release
and
proceed
or
stay behind.
The One who has gone before left behind His greatness
to fit the human form.
So long ago, He stepped through
with grace and humility.
Without His princely entourage,
His deity was disregarded,
even when His speech subdued the elements
and
His touch delivered remedy and peace.
He had to die Himself to let us in through the door to life.
When the door seemed shut for everyone,
sin
was accounted to Him
who went before to make away
for mortal men.
This One left behind His
name
for those who would
Believe and heed
the guidance He gives within.
For me there have been numerous doors,
getting smaller
all the while.
Each time I pass through,
more must be
left
behind.

Place to Draw:
Use three colored pencils to complete this picture. Apply yellow first around the edge of the door and especially at the place where the door meets the floor. Next use tan (light brown) to overlap the yellow just a bit. Dark brown is last, overlapping into the tan but not the yellow. Be sure to build up the layers of colors lightly at first, saving the bold, heavy strokes for the dark areas at the outer edges of the drawing.

Place to Write:
What is stopping you from opening the door to let light in? Write it out.

Crisis

Crisis, one after another is caused by credit without a base.
Yes that is the case.
We the people, our country have allowed wanton spending called credit on what security?
What responsibility?
"You have plowed wickedness;
You have reaped iniquity.

You have eaten the fruit of lies,
Because you trusted in your own way,
in the multitude of your mighty men."

Hosea 10:13

Place to Draw:
Take a leaf and observe it at different. Draw a rectangle or box around it. Imagine turning the box on its end and side, and draw these views. Training the eye to see proportion comes from close looking.

Place to Write:
Have you fallen down? You will not stay there. Grow out into the unknown by trusting scripture, the Word of God. Write verses here such as Ephesians 3:14–21.

Vote

Just take a poke at it!
Politics make people tic.
Without organization and order, things would get totally out of line.

Analyze the word: "Pol" is not for pole cat,

"Li" is not for lying,
And "Tic" is not what leaves when you lie so much you are good at it.

No, I'm not joking.

Go ahead and opinionate and fume, but don't forget to cast the ballot.

Place to Draw:
Put in your vote here! What color do you want as the color for the word "Vote"? Make it the color that best suits the way you feel when you exercise that right.

Place to Write:
Did the election not go your way? Write an action plan for the future and review it weekly. Do not live life as a victim! Have a realistic vision for the future.

Students, Pupils, Kids, Children
What a wonderful mixture they are.
Look out among the class about to start.

"Welcome to the classroom."
That's what each face seems say.

Do they enjoy learning?
Discovering?
Not memorizing dates and formula.

No, theirs is to find their place
In this ever-changing world

So in their faces one sees the future.
Our time is gone and the future is theirs.

What have we done to secure a place for growth?
Foundation, base, rock, stabilization,

Prayer, conversation with God will direct young and

Old to lift up this human race.
No relationship of man is stronger than with God, our Maker.

Who has the yearning, the desire to achieve?
Pray for the grace of God's leading.
Who believes that the Creator made them for a certain thing?
Seek His face when all others have no encouragement.
Who does what only they can do,
Not gauging himself by lives of others?
It is this one He who keeps in perfect peace.

In the past the young dreamed of e-mail, of satellites finding a place
on the earth the size of a flea's face.

All these concepts take time to brew.
They are seeds that need water and light.
How far go the roots of the person who makes God their light and future.

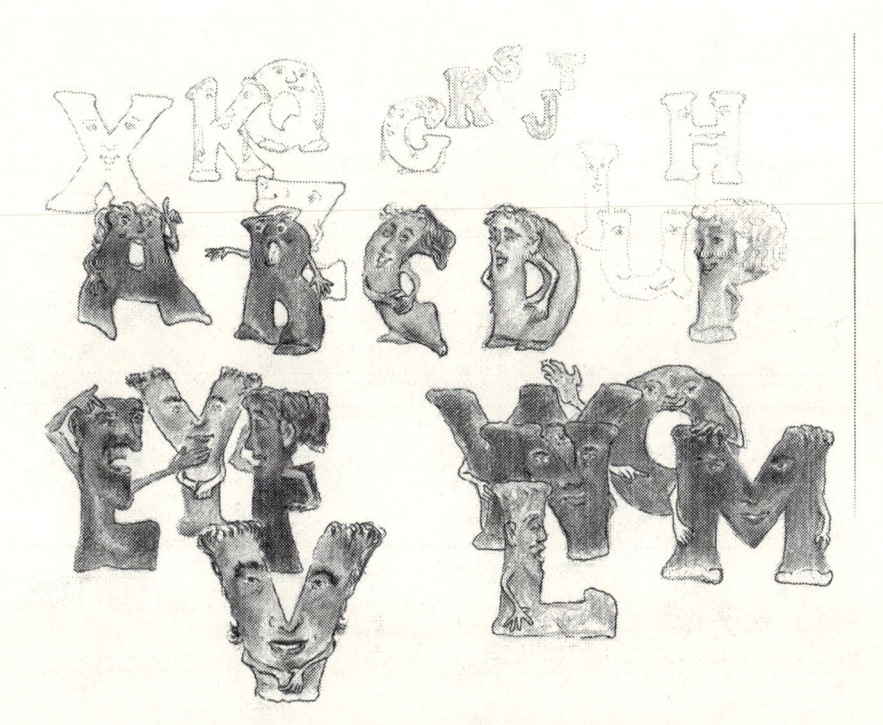

Place to Draw:
With tracing paper, trace the letters above with pencil and then change them to create a set of numbers with human characteristics.

Place to Write:
Working with groups is challenging. Before you find yourself in the front of a group, have a plan even though you may not be an organizer. It works to group a large group into smaller units by birthday, interest (dog lovers, cat lovers, etc.).
Leadership does not mean you do everything, it means you help others understand what they can do to help in a situation.

The Ultimate Relationship

Heart, Soul, and Mind

It is a long wait to understand and to be understood.
Why think to yourself all the time inside your mind?
There are places there one wishes not to unearth.
Even so, with just your view, blindness is certain, and the completeness that brings peace cannot be had.

Why stumble through this life without purpose?

A line connects this heart, this mind.

Soul, is this the line that connects heart to intelligence?
Does the soul complete me?

Bring Truth in my soul to complete me.

Creator, you know the mind and the heart.

Without soul, mind and heart cannot live in complete bond with Thee or any other.

The circle of peace is complete in the heart, the mind, and the soul when one allows the Creator to place in each secret thought His heart of hearts and His mind on each matter.

Thank you for putting within each of us a need to connect the heart to the mind.

Place to Draw:
Simplify your drawing selecting only structural lines in a room to put in first. Most rooms are a big box and at any one time you see only the top, bottom and three sides of the box. With this in mind begin by sketching the line where top and one wall meet. Next pencil in the vertical line for the side of the wall and then the vertical line for the opposite side. Walls are rectangles connected to other rectangles. Use pencil and draw lightly until you get it correct.

Place to Write:
What areas of life keep you confused and upset? Are you praying ahead of time, asking for wisdom and guidance? Christ knows our shortcomings and wants to complete us. Take time to practice feeling His presence before encountering difficult situations. Write out a prayer to meet the next encounter. Be sure to go back to this place and write out how God supplied for you in your time of need.

You Made Me to Think, You've Made Me to Know

At times, I think about the most profound things. Is there anything that hasn't been thought or said before my having said it? At this point, you often remind me that

Although King David wrote of such deep thoughts, emotions, desires, and beautiful praise of You,

Although Paul, the scholar of Your thoughts, expressed so clearly Your love for us,

You have made me to think and to know of the love You have for me, love no angel can sing of, no other being will know quite like me. You made me to know, You've made me to think of Thee, my Creator and King.

Place to Draw:
After reading Genesis, chapter one, draw your understanding of what the earth would look like "without form, and void." Go ahead and use your imagination.

Place to Write:
Is everything still "very good," as Genesis 1:31 tells us? Can we destroy what God has created? Read Revelation 1:8 and think about all that has happened since creation. What is the plan?

Truth, Freedom's Key

Upon waking one bright spring morning, dread bound me. Where was the joy of the believer? The sense of well-being was gone, and the worries of the day before held me fast. Then a thought came to me: why had I gone to bed with these lies of the day before? "You will never change; your lot in life is to be less than you could have been because you have failed."

Quickly my mind reached for the Truth, which is always with me. I sought the One who made me, who wants to guide me along the way. These worries lurked in the future and not the here and now. My judge exists in the past, present, and future.

Yes, freedom's key was there to meet with me.

I had not time to associate with the Truth until now …

Disconnected with nothing to do but search my soul.

You see, the Truth is not in me,

I must invite the Truth to come and abide in me richly.

Moment by moment,
This Person of the Cross
Regards me.
I need thee, Light.

Place to Draw:
Create space by using one line as an edge and many lines as shadow and form. Add words such as liberty, choice, and so on. Think of each letter in the word as having a top, two sides, and a bottom. The "key" is an optical mistake in that the top does not match the base in perspective. Just have fun creating letters to appear as if they are occupying space.

Place to Write:
What is keeping you from enjoying the day? Put down those things that bind you. Put them where they belong, outside you. You control what goes in your mind. Write a song or favorite scripture that will encourage you to seek the one who does control all things.

The Love Letter

How delightful it is to receive a hand-written message allowing one to enjoy the life of another. Even if it is information one already knows, the writer took time to put down thoughts to send to another.

God wrote His message to us first on the hearts of men, and to know these letters have been opened, folded, and read again and again, for loving thoughts are kept to bring fresh remembrances of the one we love.

Stories of men and women imprisoned without His letter, His word in hand testify of the peace and joy His Spirit's voice gives. With the words of the letter heard in their hearts, they are free.

What makes a message so intimate is to know the one whose the cherished thoughts. Remarks of instruction, encouragement, and care are received. A relationship exists between writer and reader.

Some people may say the letter is not personal and written directly to them, for they have not met the Word made flesh, the one who created the life they now live, the scribe of all creation's design, the master of all that is and will ever be.

Place to Draw:
Draw a landscape that includes a river and hills or mountains in the distance. Use the simple drawing on the previous page. Use pencil and finalize in black fine-point pen.

Place to Write:
Write a letter to someone you need to forgive. It may be that you have no way of delivering it, but don't let that stop you from writing. Every time the deed that you just forgave comes to mind, remind yourself of this letter.

Do You Know

How do you know
Until you find out?

How do you know until you show
That you don't

What do I have to dread
But ignorance itself?

Has God ever said,
"Don't ask!"
He may say,
"Not now"
Or
"Why do you ask?"

To the all-knowing Lord,
Who is and always shall be,
I said, "I don't know why,
And I'm afraid to ask."

The answer came to me:
"Know yourself so you can know the
all in all, Truth and Light,
Beginning and Never Ending,
Love and Life …"

To know not fear, ignorance, and doubt
When I know Him and myself.

Place to Draw:
Using three fine-point pens (red, blue, and black), color in the shapes and areas with dots and lines. Do not make any area solid, but do make dots and lines closer in some places and sparser in others.

Place to Write:
With what you know now about your life, are you satisfied, or do you long to grow beyond your current state? As many writing teachers say, "Answer in complete sentences," and even better give an argument for both sides of the opinion.

Music

Music: what is it? Notes written on a lined page to sing, strum, beat, or blow? Notations directing the rhythm, accent, volume, and duration? Music: what is it? Emotions felt long ago to be heard in truth? Sweet or sad or soft or intense notes created to celebrate and relive. Imagine with me the first crescendo of sound as the Word was spoken to direct the creation of all. "It was good!" Music is the way to live.

Place to Draw:
In the large shapes provided, draw a flow of reaped shapes or patterns. Let them get larger to give the effect of movement causing them to flow.

Place to Write:
List the names of songs you remember. Why do these songs come to mind? Make up song names for the circumstances you are now interested in.

A Song

A song I can sing; will you join in with me? The chorus we'll all sing—you, me, and those who will come along to sing the word. Christ in you, Christ in me, Christ in these we see … the harvest.

Who will roll away the stone that blocks the voice, the sound, the ears, the mind? Walk and as you go, show that you follow the one who will lead us to life everlasting. Sing the part, your part of the song. Each song rises to be heard as a symphony by He who gives the song the voice, the sound, allowing those who have ears to hear with the spirit and the truth.

The Word made flesh performs the task of love to bring joy to the broken, confused, and lost. Hallelujah and hosanna to the great I Am.

A song only we can sing; will you join in with us? The chorus we'll all sing—you, me, and those who will come along to sing the word. Christ in you, Christ in me, Christ in these we see … the harvest.

Place to Draw:
Finish the street drawing by adding people doing everyday things, such as walking a dog, reading a newspaper while waiting for a bus, or window shopping.

Place to Write:
Scripture tells us that the "field is white unto harvest" and that the Christians are called to labor with Him, not for Him. How many times have you wanted Christ to be there with you? He is; trust and obey, and you will know the gift of His presence. Describe a circumstance that needs you to walk out in Christ.

Suggested Reading:

The Holy Bible. Any version that you enjoy; there are so many.
Boundaries, by Dr. Henry Cloud and Dr. John Townsend
Weather of the Heart, by Madeleine L'Engle
In His Image, by Philip Yancey and Paul Brand